IMAGES
*of America*

# WATERTOWN ARSENAL

This building, known as the laboratory, was constructed in 1842 in the Greek Revival style. It was demolished early in the 20th century. Judging by the timbers protruding from underneath the porch, it appears that the structure had just been moved, or was about to be moved, in this undated image.

*On the cover*: A lone worker is dwarfed by a giant gear-cutting machine in this early-20th-century view. (Courtesy National Archives and Records Administration.)

IMAGES
*of America*

# WATERTOWN ARSENAL

Alan R. Earls

ARCADIA
PUBLISHING

This image of the North Storehouse shows the stone inset indicating the date of construction—the year the arsenal was commenced at Watertown.

# CONTENTS

# ACKNOWLEDGMENTS

In assembling this book and writing the text, I have received tremendous assistance from Joan Gearin and the rest of the staff of the National Archive in Waltham, Massachusetts. Gearin's 2006 lecture about the Watertown Arsenal at the Watertown Historical Society provided a terrific introduction to the topic, and her knowledge of the resources under her care was immense. All the images contained in this book, with two exceptions noted in text, came from the Watertown Arsenal by way of the National Archive. I am also greatly in debt to Judy D. Dobbs, author of *A History of the Watertown Arsenal, 1816–1967*, published in 1977 by the Army Materials and Mechanics Research Center. Her carefully researched text is a treasure trove of facts. Other published sources consulted in the preparation of this work include *Scientific Management in Action: Taylorism at Watertown Arsenal, 1908–1915* by Hugh G. J. Aitken and *History of the Watertown Arsenal*, a video produced in 1994 by Robert and Thomas Greim.

# INTRODUCTION

For most of the thousands of people who drive down Arsenal Street in Watertown, its name is probably a cipher, and the architecture unremarkable. But a closer look still reveals the traces of a historically important enterprise—the Watertown Arsenal—which played a key role in the defense of the nation from shortly after the War of 1812 until the peak of the Vietnam War (and beyond, if one counts the smaller research organizations such as the Army Materials and Mechanics Research Center that succeeded it). Traces of the rail line that once supplied steel, coal, and oil to the foundry operations—and rolled away bearing gigantic artillery—can be seen in several places. Upon closer inspection, some of the brick buildings reveal architectural details that betray their long history.

Greater Boston originally had an arsenal located in Charlestown, but when it became desirable to expand the navy yard there, the U.S. Army had to find a new home. Watertown was selected because it was inland but still reachable by ship (in the days before the damming of the Charles River). Initially the Watertown Arsenal was little more than a depot at which some guns were stored, built, or repaired. Over the course of time, however, the Watertown Arsenal evolved into a place where important innovations in armaments and metallurgy would occur.

For example, the Watertown Arsenal commander (1859–1865) Thomas J. Rodman, began experiments that led, after much delay by the hidebound ordnance establishment, to the implementation of his casting process that involved a phased cooling of the gun barrel from the inside out, so that the outer parts would shrink tightly over the inner, resulting in greater strength. His giant Rodman cannon were an important weapon in the Civil War, and his methods were quickly adopted in Europe. Rodman subsequently capped his career by helping to establish the Rock Island Arsenal in Illinois.

Rodman's permanent legacy was his focus on metallurgy and innovation. Through war and peace, the Watertown Arsenal remained at the forefront of this field for the remainder of its history.

The Watertown Arsenal was established initially with the purchase of 20 acres of land for the bargain, in modern terms, of just over $2,000. Other purchases followed. By 1819, a quadrangle of structures with more than a dozen buildings was taking shape beside the Charles River. In most cases, structures were made with attention to detail, so that many of the original structures served through the entire history of the Watertown Arsenal and continue in other uses today. At least five soldiers were killed in the construction, according to a memorial tablet in a Watertown cemetery.

A carpenter shop and blacksmithing facility were also established almost immediately. A laboratory was also put in place, although its focus was more on tasks such as mixing paint or lubricants than on the research activities that one might expect.

Following the Mexican War, large quantities of gunpowder and supplies were shipped to Watertown for storage—and in some cases, reuse during the Civil War. In that later conflict, employment exceeded 600 by 1863—with more than 10 percent of the work force being female. By the end of the war, employment exceeded 800, including more than 100 women.

Like the rest of the U.S. military establishment, activities at the Watertown Arsenal tapered off dramatically after Appomattox, but not for long. Despite a proposal by Congress in 1884 to close the Watertown Arsenal—at which point 14 officers and 194 (male) civilians were employed—the years between Abraham Lincoln and Woodrow Wilson saw both a qualitative and quantitative expansion in the facility's products. One of the most notable milestones was the design and completion of the Emery Testing Machine, built by Ames Manufacturing Company of Chicopee Falls. This pioneering device, still emulated by a succession of more modern machines around the world, could test metal samples under a compression load of one million pounds and a tension load of 800,000 pounds. Significantly the Emery Testing Machine, could also be switched over to test very light load or tensions, providing a full spectrum of metallurgical information.

These were years of great scientific progress everywhere, as well as revolutionary developments in armaments. Breechloading weapons began to replace traditional muzzle loaders in everything from small arms to the giant coast defense and field artillery that was increasingly the focus of work at Watertown. Iron and bronze were increasingly supplanted by steel alloys. Carriages for field guns, railroad guns, and fixed fortress artillery were made of metal and often incorporated complex gearing, loading mechanism, and even armor.

As the United States passed through the Gilded Age, its role as a world power and industrial titan came into focus, and the Watertown Arsenal seemed to have been in step with the times. Even management methods were being scrutinized for improvement. In a famous incident, Frederick Winslow Taylor, often described as the "father of scientific management," applied his time and motion study methods to work at the Watertown Arsenal, examining the minutest aspects of the way workers performed their jobs in an effort to devise an ideal method, which would thereafter be imposed on all. His activities, however, precipitated a 1911 strike. A later court case determined that Taylor's methods would not be permitted at federal sites.

The rest of the history of the Watertown Arsenal is full of stories of innovation. For instance, the adoption and improvement of autofrettage methods (strain hardening) helped ensure that American gun barrels were stronger and lasted longer.

Walter S. Baird, a Harvard professor, and John Sterner, who together founded Baird Associates in 1937 (a pioneering high tech firm), had an affiliation with the Watertown Arsenal. Their company created the market for spectrographic analysis equipment. Others were leaders in using radiological methods to better understand metals.

Of course, research only occupied a fraction of the work force directly. Most of the Watertown Arsenal was focused on broad-shouldered work of the smoke and flame variety. In 1940, when a celebration marked the Watertown Arsenal's 125 years, 5,000 employees were present. In 1942, 6,000 attended the Army-Navy E Award ceremony, and almost 10,000 were employed by the end of that year.

With the Cold War came new challenges and new technologies. The giant Atomic Cannon was one project that absorbed the attention of the Watertown Arsenal (one of these giant guns was even part of Pres. Dwight Eisenhower's first inaugural parade).

Although the Watertown Arsenal faded from view after its 1967 closure, it did not disappear. Army research activities occupied a section of the property until the late 1980s. Of course, many of the buildings associated with the Watertown Arsenal have gone on to serve new and important functions as the Watertown Arsenal Mall, offices, and research spaces. Sadly one of the Watertown Arsenal's legacies has been pollution—something it has in common with many older industrial and military sites. However as the pictures here show, the Watertown Arsenal was also about people—thousands of people from Watertown and surrounding communities who built their careers and their families around this important American institution.

# One

# THE EARLY YEARS OF THE WATERTOWN ARSENAL

Cap. George Talcott, first commanding officer of the Watertown Arsenal from 1816 to 1820, was instrumental in selecting the site and in fending off attempts to locate elsewhere, such as Portsmouth, New Hampshire. He later rose to be chief of the Ordnance Department of the U.S. Army (1848–1851).

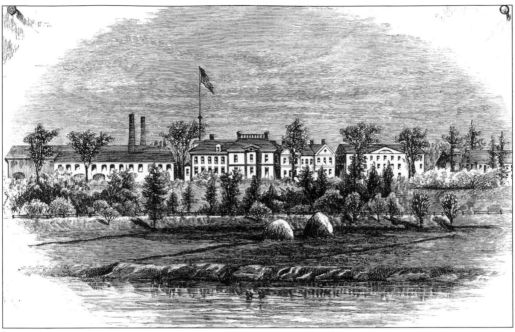

This print of a sketch of the Watertown Arsenal from the late 1860s shows the extent of development during the facility's early decades.

REPRESENTATION OF THE MAGAZINE, ETC., OF THE ARSENAL, AT WATERTOWN, MASS.
BOSTON, SATURDAY, AUGUST 6 1853

W.A.921-201

The stone magazine here was built in 1817 and is shown as the artist viewed it on a Saturday in 1817. Note the visitors and a passing workman mingling with the soldiers on guard duty.

That same Saturday, the artist sketched this scene showing the officers' quarters at the Watertown Arsenal. With many of its buildings designed by architect Alexander Parris, the Watertown Arsenal resembled some of the finest neighborhoods in New England more than it did a utilitarian military site.

EXTERIOR VIEW OF THE UNITED STATES ARSENAL, AT WATERTOWN, MASS.

A view from 1856 shows a bridge along the Charles River connecting Watertown and Brighton, with the Watertown Arsenal in the background. Once again, the easy familiarity between soldier and civilian is shown by the boaters and the passing carriage.

This Harpers Weekly cover, dated July 20, 1861, only two months after the Confederate bombardment of Fort Sumter began the hostilities of the Civil War, shows men and women working to prepare cartridges for the Union Army at Watertown. It would not be the last time that women swelled the workforce in time of war.

Abraham Lincoln doubtless appreciated the tremendous output of the Watertown Arsenal during the Civil War, but although the character at the left in this photograph bears a resemblance to the 16th president, it is actually an image of Lt. Col. T. S. Laidley (later a commander at Watertown) at Fort Monroe in Virginia in the late 1860s, after the Civil War. The other men are not identified. The gun was a 15-inch Rodman weighing about 25 tons and firing a 300-pound shell.

This photograph captures the Watertown Arsenal and its still-pastoral setting late in the 19th century.

Probably taken in the 1870s, this image shows the Iron and Brass Foundry erected after the Civil War along the river, adjacent to the gashouse. The wharf and schooner give evidence as to why Watertown was considered an ideal location. Although a safe distance from the coast, it could still be reached by ship.

This undated image may date back to the Civil War period, judging by both the type of ordnance on display and by its quantity.

With their ornate M1881 felt helmets, these soldiers date this picture of the Watertown Arsenal to the late 19th century, when cannon balls, like those stacked in the foreground, were approaching obsolescence.

*Two*

# GROWTH AND
# THE GREAT WAR

The officers' quarters, as shown here, were photographed in 1909.

In addition to the research and industrial activity, the Watertown Arsenal often had at least a few children in residence. These three seem to be enjoying the lush surroundings.

This summery view shows the officers' quarters with the porch removed.

Constructed in 1905, the enlisted men's barracks was designed to accommodate 75. Later it also served as an officers' club.

This 1910 view is described in the National Archives as "a general view of the shops." A careful examination of the right hand side of the image reveals the giant pulleys protruding from the ends of the buildings. These pulleys, along with equally substantial belts, provided power to the machinery inside.

In the days before computerization, scale models were an important way to verify the feasibility of designs prior to commencing manufacture. This is a model of a disappearing gun carriage in the raised (or firing) position.

The same model shown above is shown here in its lowered position, designed to shelter behind the stone, concrete, and earth of a coast fort. The model even includes the equipment used for loading the gun.

The real thing is seen here. This image shows a 10-inch disappearing carriage gun being fired at Fort Warren in Boston Harbor. Note the man in the foreground trying to protect his ears.

Seen here is another large-caliber, disappearing carriage gun in the lowered position.

A 10-inch mortar and carriage is being assembled in this Watertown Arsenal photograph.

This 1907 photograph shows an elaborate machine devised to test the recoil cylinders of artillery pieces, such as the one at left, apparently through an impact with a large, rolling wheel.

This 1913 image shows the man in the foreground about to pull the lanyard to fire an experimental long-recoil 3-inch field gun.

The same type of gun shown above is caught at its maximum recoil, just after firing.

Two Watertown Arsenal employees pose here with a 12-inch mortar—probably destined for a coast-defense installation—in this interior image. The massiveness of the mount is easy to see.

A 16-inch gun, model 1895, dwarfs the two men that stand beside it. Note the rollers between the layers of supporting timbers for moving the gun.

As the sign in this photograph states, this gun was intended for shooting down enemy observation balloons, the chief aerial threat at a time when fixed-wing aircraft were still viewed as novelties. The clever mechanical arrangement shown here allows the road wheels to be deployed to permit rapid traverse of the gun.

BALLOON GUN CARRIAGE,
MODEL OF 1910

This is another variation on the disappearing carriage. In this case, the massive counterweight apparently helps with recoil and with raising and lowering the gun.

A Watertown-built 7-inch siege howitzer is shown here with full livery.

These soldiers and their horses seem to have been defeated by every army's enemy: mud. The gun appears similar to the howitzer shown above but without spoked wheels.

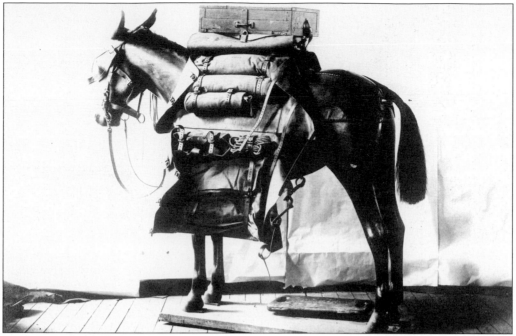

Draft animals fulfilled many roles in the army well into the 20th century. This image shows a full-size model encumbered with a complex equipment kit. The same group of photographs at the archive included another unfortunate model mule standing in a field but without its head—a sight that must have puzzled passersby.

This close up provides a gunner's-eye view of a 6-inch barbette-type gun mount, taken in 1915. The thickness of the armor, perhaps two inches, can be easily judged.

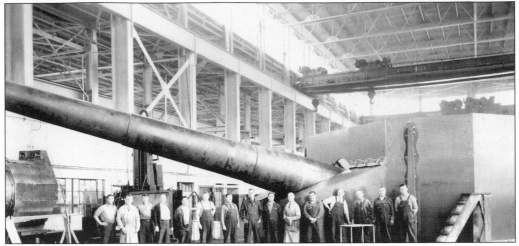

This striking image shows a workforce dwarfed by a barbette mount and its 16-inch gun. The greater protection for gun and crew provided by the barbette became increasingly important as guns achieved longer ranges and adopted indirect fire methods, which could bring an enemy shell arcing down from above.

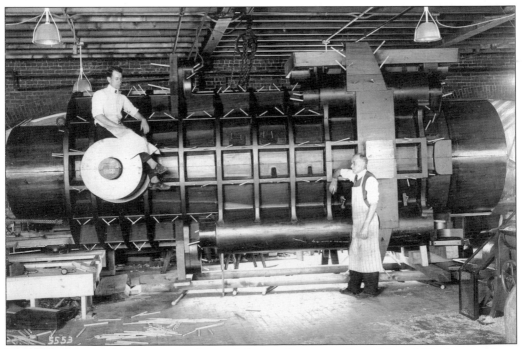

This 1919 photograph shows two workers and the wooden pattern for making a 16-inch gun mount.

These literally man-sized objects were the business end, so to speak, of the huge guns crafted at the Watertown Arsenal. The "HE" stands for high-explosive, "DP" stands for deep penetration, while "AP" stands for armor piercing, which had reduced explosive power but plenty of kinetic energy and a tip of hardened steel.

Building 311 is shown here in 1918 with a 16-inch railway gun under construction.

Another 1918 view of building 311 shows stacks of artillery shells on the left side of the image, probably for the 16-inch gun.

Civilian life goes on in the background of this image, which shows another 16-inch railway gun. Note the massive support needed, 16 axles front and rear. In the middle, men are cranking down stabilizers, which would need to be in place to fire the weapon.

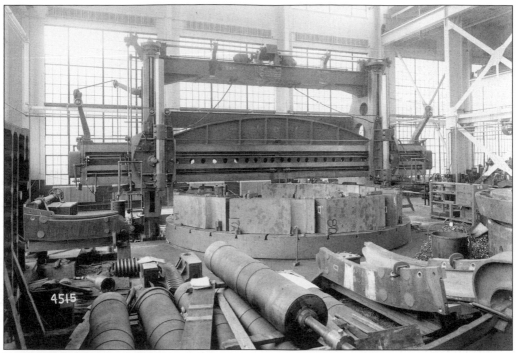

This giant boring mill would probably have been used in the manufacture of large artillery gun barrels.

This is the test specimen shop during the World War I period. Science and engineering were always closely allied with output at the Watertown Arsenal.

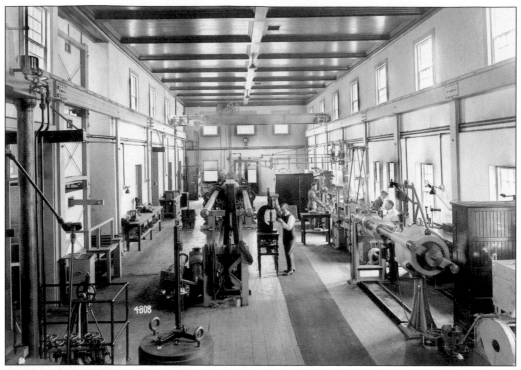

This photograph shows the test laboratories, with the Emery Testing Machine on the right.

This is a group of Watertown Arsenal employees with a pouring ingot. Judging by the narrow, catwalk with no railing, safety was not a high priority.

Shown here is the model 59½ press manufactured by the Toledo Machine and Tool Company of Toledo and a crew of Watertown Arsenal men.

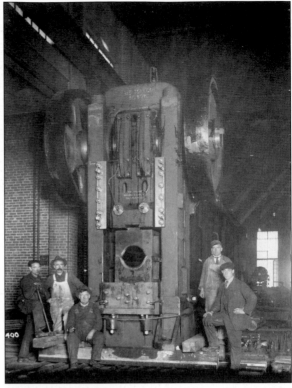

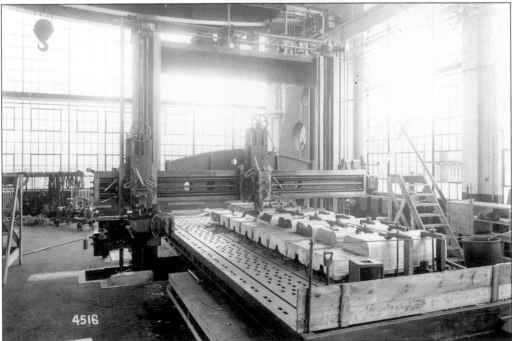

The huge piece of equipment in the foreground of this 1918 photograph is a planer. Machining operations at the Watertown Arsenal were on a scale unlike almost anything else in the region's industry.

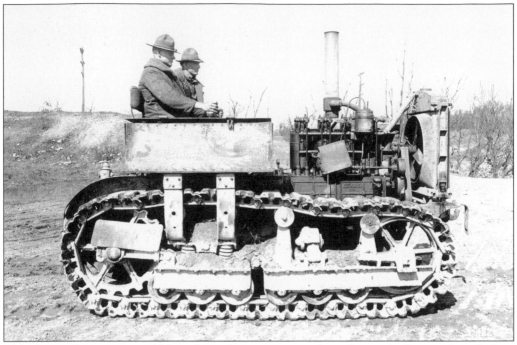

This Caterpillar tractor could have been the successor to the unhappy draft animals with their mired howitzer, shown on page 24. The Watertown Arsenal was often a force for innovation.

Seen here are a World War I 240-millimeter gun carriage and limber, adjacent to the arsenal—all towed by a single vehicle, possibly a Nash Quad, one of the first four-wheel drive trucks, used widely be the army. Note the application of camouflage schemes on all of the equipment.

This Knox chain-drive pumper, reportedly manufactured in Boston, marked the Watertown Arsenal fire department as very up-to-date.

While primitive in appearance compared to modern apparatus, the Knox pumper could put up an impressive volume of water as seen in this demonstration.

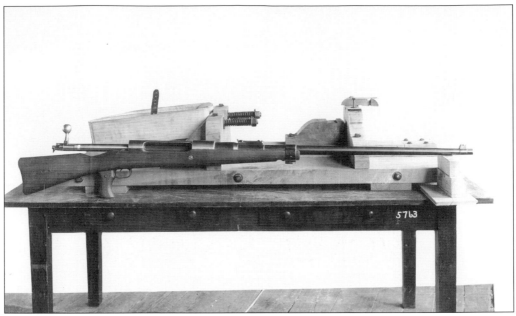

Another role that the Watertown Arsenal fulfilled was evaluating foreign military equipment. This setup shows a 13-millimeter German antitank rifle in a test fixture. These weapons were somewhat unwieldy but could be very effective against the thinly-armored World War I tanks.

This shot, from 1920, just two years after the war, shows a Vickers 8-inch howitzer platform wagon from England. A light tank, probably either a French Renault or an American made version, can be seen in the background.

# *Three*

# WOMEN'S WORK

Two women appear to be checking stock among the parts bins at the Watertown Arsenal in this image. Women moved into a wider range of jobs than ever before at the Watertown Arsenal during World War I.

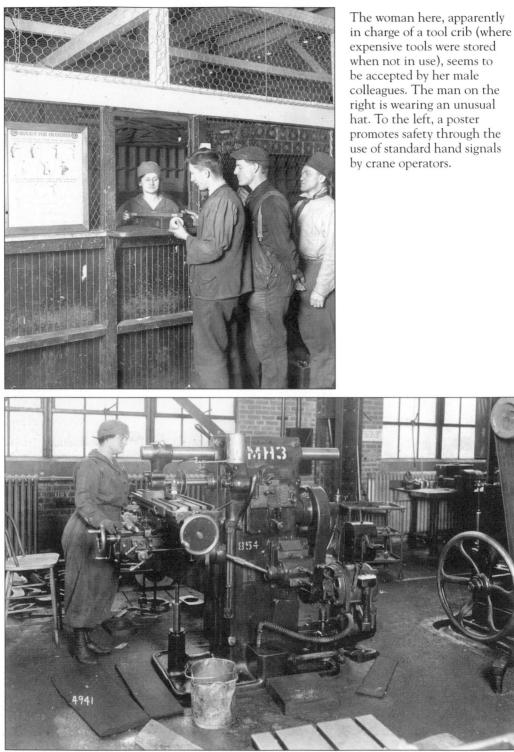

The woman here, apparently in charge of a tool crib (where expensive tools were stored when not in use), seems to be accepted by her male colleagues. The man on the right is wearing an unusual hat. To the left, a poster promotes safety through the use of standard hand signals by crane operators.

This woman is operating a milling machine. Judging by the number of women operating similar equipment, many women must have mastered the skills required in a short time.

This image is titled "Women Operators in the Projectile Shop," although the person on the right appears to be a man. Some machines at this date had their own electrical motors. Those in this image retain the overhead belting, which made for a noisier and potential more dangerous work place.

This woman is prudently keeping a safe distance from the blade of this metal-cutting machine. The warning sign on the brick wall is written in both English and Italian—a clue to the ethnic makeup of the workforce at the time.

Women (both black and white) have cleanup duties in this photograph. They appear to be sweeping up wood shavings, which may have been used to soak up spilled cutting oil.

These women seem to be tackling a shipping/receiving task. The windows toward the rear can be opened as a unit through a mechanical arrangement. Windows of this type were common in industrial settings.

This woman is operating a shaper, which was a special type of milling machine, sometimes equipped with several cutters and heads to mill various surfaces.

The women who worked as machinists at the Watertown Arsenal went through this Training School. The large machine in the background and to the right is a Woodward and Powell, manufactured in Worcester. For many years, New England firms were a dominant force in the machine tool business.

These women (in the background) are operating what appear to be very large lathes, probably for finishing gun barrels.

This woman appears to be operating a milling machine or drill. In the foreground is what appears to be a stack of complete pieces.

"Women operators, bench work" is the description attached to this image. The woman in the center appears to be trimming some kind of gasket material with scissors.

This woman has been tasked to operate one of the many overhead cranes at the Watertown Arsenal. Behind her on her work platform is an electrical panel. Below her, one can see machine tools and gun barrels.

In the background, one can see a Shaw 10-ton overhead crane. In the foreground, suspended by another unseen overhead crane, is a large steel ingot. The casting pit can be glimpsed beneath.

## *Four*

# The Interwar Years and World War II

Student-officers from the Watertown Arsenal pose at the Massachusetts Institute of Technology (MIT) in this photograph dated May 1, 1923, somewhat late in the season for the quantity of snow visible on the steps of 77 Massachusetts Avenue. The Watertown Arsenal maintained a long-standing relationship with MIT.

One of the problems with peace was what to do with all the leftovers of war. This room, apparently put aside for storage, contains a veritable potpourri of furniture, tools, and even large caliber projectiles.

Student officers at the Watertown Arsenal are shown in this image dated July 1, 1922.

The kind of saw shown in this image would have made a good prop for *The Perils of Pauline*.

The X-ray laboratory at the Watertown Arsenal was photographed here on October 11, 1922. The Watertown Arsenal was at the forefront of materials science, in particular, developing and applying new methods of analysis. Boxes on the top shelf contain X-ray tubes.

The army headgear makes an odd contrast with the coverall worn by this man. But hands-on work also made for proficiency in the technologies used at the Watertown Arsenal.

Officers at the Watertown Arsenal appear at first glance to be operating a switchboard, but more likely this was a lab bench with electrical equipment, notebooks, and instruments.

Army enlisted men appear to be tackling all the assembly tasks on this gun mount in this photograph from the 1920s. A plank in the foreground provides access to the area of the barbette on which the men are working.

Student officers are mixed with civilian employees in this group photograph from April 1922. Railroad tracks, providing access to the interior of the building, can be seen in the center foreground.

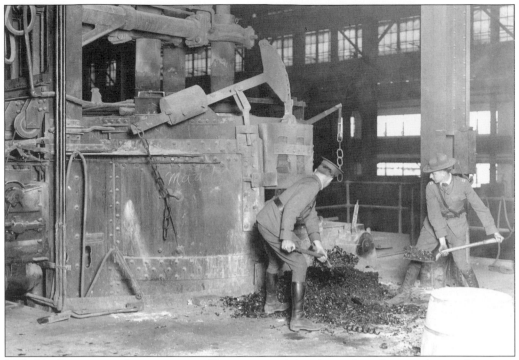

Probably few posts in the army gave officers responsibility for work as dirty as this—adding raw material to an electric foundry furnace in this case.

Enlisted men and a civilian worker are pictured here in the early 1920s at work with molds for casting large parts at the Watertown Arsenal foundry.

It must have been a sunny day, late in 1918, when this image of the maintenance shops was taken. Most of the industrial buildings depended on natural light from skylights.

Accidents were a constant problem at the Watertown Arsenal. In this photograph, a 60-foot boom from the No. 4 Brown hoisting crane is shown after its failure in an image taken September 12, 1920.

This 1919 image shows the recreation building. Railroad tracks pass just in front of the building.

The modern administration building was constructed in 1900 for a cost of $15,000. It was expanded during World War I and again during World War II. It is shown here in 1919. The plans were also used subsequently to build identical structures at Picatinny Arsenal and the Frankford Arsenal.

The center of this image, in the background, is a temporary barracks structure built for World War I. There appears to be enough lumber in the foreground to construct a similar building.

This post–World War I view shows the exterior of the forge shop. Some of the plantings in the foreground resemble cabbages, perhaps the remnants of a war garden (known during World War II as a victory garden).

This photograph is described as the "rough machine shop." The description may not fit, but it certainly seems to be a shop for machining large objects.

This excellent view is described as "super gun turning and boring lathe" and does indeed seem able to handle the manufacture of very large gun barrels.

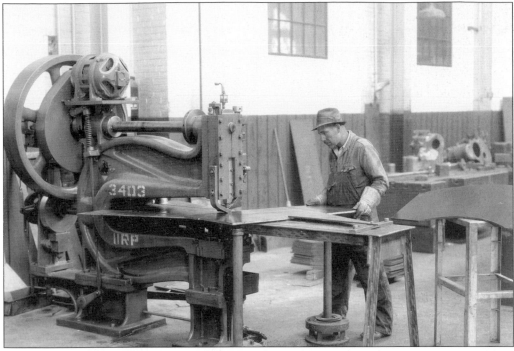

In this 1936 image, a worker concentrates on operating a nibbler to cut a sheet of half-inch Monel, a corrosion resistant steel alloy that was difficult to cut or machine conventionally.

A large gun tube completely fills this Baltimore and Ohio Railroad flatcar in this undated image.

This 1942 image, looking west, shows new track being installed and building 41 under construction in the background.

This photograph, from just before World War II, shows one of the special rail cars used to insert and remove metal items, probably parts for gun carriages, from a giant heat treating oven. The process strengthened the metal and enhanced service life. Notice the stack of bricks to the left, used to roughly seal the oven opening.

This undated image shows a physical testing laboratory, including the one million pound Emery Testing Machine in the center of the background.

The commanding general and his staff pose for the photographer in this image from 1942.

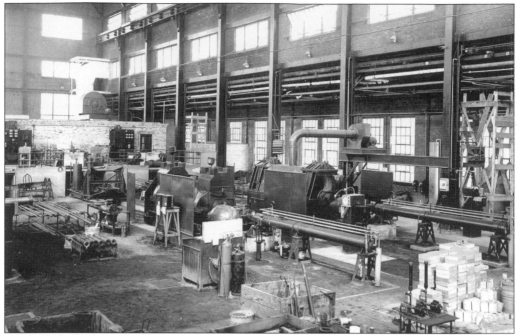

On March 14, 1940, the photographer snapped this image of what is supposed to be the physical testing laboratory in building 71.

Three-inch antiaircraft guns are being assembled in building 36 in this photograph from March 1937.

A 37-millimeter antiaircraft gun is shown in traveling position, with the gun depressed and outriggers stowed.

This is the new foundry, looking east, photographed during alterations in October 1939.

This photograph shows the early stages of construction for building 74, looking northeast, on January 27, 1942.

A similar scene is shown here, also looking northeast, but about a month after the previous image.

In a scene reminiscent of the children's book *Mike Mulligan and His Steam Shovel*, a power shovel is digging the foundation for building 74 on December 23, 1941.

Here is another construction scene—building 42—with the boom of a power shovel barely visible in the foreground. The image is from March 1942.

This is another view of building 41 construction, dated to late 1941.

Women were back in the workforce with the advent of World War II. Here the woman at the right points to a blood donor honor roll.

Let them eat cake! On an occasion unknown, this jovial bunch seems intent on enjoying a bite to eat.

This group of seven women seem to be enforcing the No Passing sign on the wall.

This unusually well photographed image shows a woman machinist at work during World War II.

These two women, both wearing photograph identification badges, seem to be focused on their work. It is possible that the glasses worn in this photograph and the image above are actually safety glasses, which became more commonplace in machine shops between the wars.

Here women are at leisure playing horseshoes in a bit of space between railroad tracks at the Watertown Arsenal.

Gentlemen played horseshoes too. This horseshoe was caught in mid-flight by the photographer.

Camaraderie is evident in this image of two Watertown Arsenal workmen during World War II.

The identities of the civilian and military men in this photograph are not recorded, but in and out of uniform, both groups had a long history of successful cooperation at the Watertown Arsenal.

Seen here is a man at work. Despite the draft, the Watertown Arsenal continued to employ many men throughout the war.

A man with a micrometer checks the dimensions of an item being manufactured.

This group of four men seems to be entirely focused on whatever is printed on the paper held by the man seated at the desk.

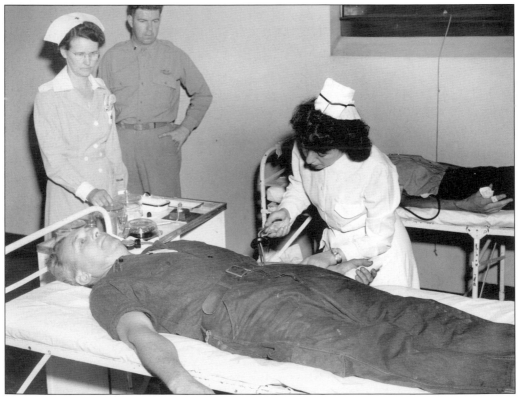

Two volunteers are shown here donating blood at a Watertown Arsenal blood drive.

Pres. Franklin D. Roosevelt can be seen seated at the back of his open touring car at the Watertown Arsenal. He visited on August 10, 1940.

Roosevelt, to the left, is seated with Boston native Frank Knox, a Republican, whom he had just appointed secretary of the navy, and Sen. David I. Walsh, a prominent isolationist. At the time, Roosevelt was trying to build bipartisan support for defense measures.

The civilian employee shown here, identified as Dr. Beeukes, was photographed July 1, 1944.

Harold Jensen, a civilian employee, was also known by his amateur radio call sign, W1KLY, which is displayed on his lapel pin. Jensen was present in 1938 when the vote was taken to establish the Waltham Amateur Radio Association, a group that is still active in the area.

This photograph shows Lt. Col. F. C. Crotty, an officer at the Watertown Arsenal during World War II.

Col. P. W. Scheidecker is seated at his desk in this wartime image. An inexpensive metal ashtray, a nearly universal desk item years ago, sits next to his telephone.

DISTINGUISHED SERVICE CROSS PURPLE HEART LEGION OF MERIT CROIX DE GUERRE

These are the medals won by Lt. Raymond W. Braffitt, the son of a Watertown Arsenal employee. Medals include the Distinguished Service Cross, Purple Heart, Legion of Merit, and Croix de Guerre.

A truck has been pressed into service as a stage for a program at which the medals awarded to Lt. Raymond W. Braffitt were presented posthumously to his father, James M. Braffitt of the Service Division.

Col. John Mather (left), commanding officer of the Watertown Arsenal, greets Rangers and Alamo Scouts, from left to right, Maj. Alexander Smith, public relations officer of First Service Command; Capt. Robert W. Prince; Captain Daxe; Pfc. Leland A. Provencher; Pfc. Carlton Dietzel; and Sgt. Harold Hard. The group told of their experience when they rescued more than 500 prisoners held by the Japanese on Luzon. Seaman Joseph Moran, one of those liberated, is at the extreme right.

A group sharing a meal is depicted in this image, perhaps in the officers' mess hall. The two men shown in the lower image on page 64 can be seen seated to the right, facing the camera.

A Gleason Gear Cutter is seen here. This is a later view of the machine seen on the cover of this book.

The line drawing on the cover of this commemorative brochure from the 1940s, shows the 3,000 kilogram-meter Charpy Impact Machine that was first installed at the Watertown Arsenal around 1918. It helped with pioneering studies of impacts upon metal and led to the deployment of tougher steel alloys during the war. (Author's collection.)

Lest anyone forget the purpose the work at the Watertown Arsenal or the importance of funding that work, this sign, with the caricature of Adolph Hitler, would remind them.

Watertown Arsenal laboratory personnel were photographed in May 1939. According to the caption written on the back of this image, they are, from left to right, Dr. E. L. Reed, W. P. Galvin, W. K. Murray, W. L. Warner, Dr. H. H. Lester, M. G. Yatsevitch, S. Vigo, M. O. Snyder, H. G. Carter, F. L. Brackley, J. Cavanagh, H. C. Knowlton, Dr. P. R. Kosting, T. K. Zagwin, Major Barry, A. Squires, Ethel M. Girard, Dr. J. L. Martin, Doris Sweeney, David Low, A. Sloan, Gertrude Frey, N. L. Reed, Maj. G. L. Guion, Mary Murphy, Kay Healy, T. E. Woodward, Mary R. Norton, Alice Raferty, J. J. Manion, J. McDermott, R. D. Chandler, Frances O'Halloran, Martha Guber, D. E. Driscoll, John P. Stecke, Shea LaBonte, Mrs. Williams, and H. L. Phillips (directly behind Major Barry, John Sterner).

Members of the Ordnance School were photographed on May 24, 1940. Members of the group from left to right are (first row) 2nd Lt. E. N. Kirsten, O.D.; 1sts Lt. E. D. Mohlere, O.D.; Prof. C. E. Fuller, dean of army students at MIT; Col. R. W. Case, O.D., arsenal commander; Maj. S. B. Ritchie, O.D., school officer; Capt. E. S. Mathews O.D.; and 2nd Lt. O. G. Kreiser, Inf.; (second row) 1st Lt. P. P. Bernd, Inf.; 1st Lt. W. F. Meaney, O.D.; 1st Lt. J. L. Cowhey, O.D.; 2nd Lt. J. S. Brierley, Inf.; 1st Lt. J. S. Luckett, Inf.; 1st Lt. R. V. Dickson, Inf.; 1st Lt. A. V. Dishman, O.D.; 1st Lt. W. Mencher, O.D.; 1st Lt. A. W. Manlove, O.D.; and 2nd Lt. S. W. Connelly, Inf.; (third row) 1st Lt. P. H. Brown, O.D.; 1st Lt. J. L. McGehee, O.D.; 1st Lt. M. L. DeGuire, O.D.; 1st Lt. E. G. Robbins Jr., F.A.; 2nd Lt. A. B. Robbins Jr., F.A.; 1st Lt. F. G. Crabb Jr., Inf.; and 1st Lt. C. H. Wood, Inf.

The Inspector School, class of 1940, flanked by 19th-century mortars, was photographed on October 29, 1940. They are F. L. Miller (1); J. M. Russell (2); T. W. Meisenzahl (3); Lt. I. H. Comroe, in charge (4); C. B. Shea (5); Col. R. W. Case, C.O. (6); G. R. Ross (7); M. B. Hassett, chief inspector (8); C. R. DeMallie (9); E. L. Roscher (10); W. O. Clemson (11); E. A. Coan (12); F. H. Brysacz (13); R. W. Kolb (14); R. V. Plichta (15); M. T. Jerkovich (16); E. F. Glesmann (17); J. S. Noragon (18); P. C. Williamson (19); J. J. Warga (20); M. M. Klein (21); J. K. Dysart (22); F. B. Litton (23); G. F. Dolan (24); L. E. Canfield (25); N. G. Anderson (26); R. R. Hill (27); J. F. Durning (28); D. W. Gotshell (29); A. J. Nuss (30); G. R. Fulton (31); M. W. Koldansky (32); M. W. Roberts (33); A. A. Dow (34); J. Quirk (35); and J. B. Collins (36).

This group is the members of the Reserve Officer's School, photographed July 14, 1940. They are, from left to right, (first row) Lt. Col. D. A. Lenk, O.R. instructor; Lt. Col. C. G. Young, O.D., assistant to the C.O.; Col. R. W. Case, O.D., commanding officer; Lt. Col. A. Vesey, O.R., in charge of the school; Maj. G. W. Foote, O.R.; and Maj. R. L. Goetzenberger, O.R.; (second row) 1st Lt. L. F. Unger, O.R.; Capt. D. H. Pletta, O.R.; Capt. R. VanVliet, O.R.; Capt. J. J. Ferri, O.R.; Capt. W. H. Mellen, O.R.; and 1st Lt. V. L. Parsegian, O.R.; (third row) 1st Lt. M. L. Lazear, O.R.; Second Lieutenant Nickerson, O.R.; 1st Lt. G. R. Fugal, O.R.; and 2nd Lt. S. J. Czyzak, O.R.

The Watertown Arsenal's security guards were photographed on August 10, 1940. They are, from left to right, (first row) A. H. Bittrich; W. H. Watts; C. R. Forguites; A. J. Williams; F. J. Concannon; Chief H. L. Havender; 1st Lt. C. F. Buck Jr., O.D.; Asst. Chief J. P. McDonough; J. Lettieri; P. J. Doonnolly; F. R. Russell; A. H. Starke; and F. A. Brouillette; (second row) H. S. Holton; J. R. Barr; F. E. Connorton; D. M. Tracy; T. Meagher; D. J. Carberry; R. J. Hanrahan; F. Krasco; T. D. Bard; and C. D. R. Peterson.

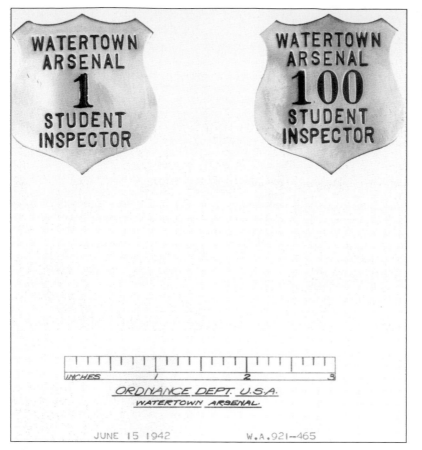

This illustration shows the design for badges for Watertown Arsenal inspectors from 1942.

Accidents continued to happen at the Watertown Arsenal. Here a gun-tube transfer trailer has broken through a tunnel cover in building 44 on May 22, 1942.

In this serious accident, a transfer car with blocking is shown. The 90-millimeter gun barrel lying adjacent to the box had pinned a man to the floor in March 1942. An artist has superimposed a line drawing of the accident process.

Magnaflux testing of a 3-inch gun barrel is performed here. The magnaflux process could reveal microscopic cracks and imperfections through the application of a strong magnetic field.

Employees here are walking to the Army-Navy E Award gathering in 1942. The Army-Navy E Award program recognized quality and productivity at defense plants.

The size and composition of the Watertown Arsenal work force can be glimpsed in this image from the Army-Navy E Award event.

An army band unit was on hand for the Army-Navy E Award celebration.

These women seem to have found a more comfortable spot, away from the crowd, from which to observe the proceedings.

Speeches by army brass at a bunting-wrapped lectern were the center point of the Army-Navy E Award event.

Here a civilian seems to have been recognized for his contributions to the Watertown Arsenal's successes.

Later in the war, certificates of commendation were given to a number of employees.

Despite the cold and snow, the band came out in full force for this occasion too.

This undated image shows a Baldwin hydraulic press of massive proportions dwarfing its operator.

Is it quitting time? This looks like an image of workers heading for the time clock to punch out.

This photograph records the results of a hydraulic test on a 76-millimeter gun barrel section. The interior rifling is clearly visible where a large wall section has broken off.

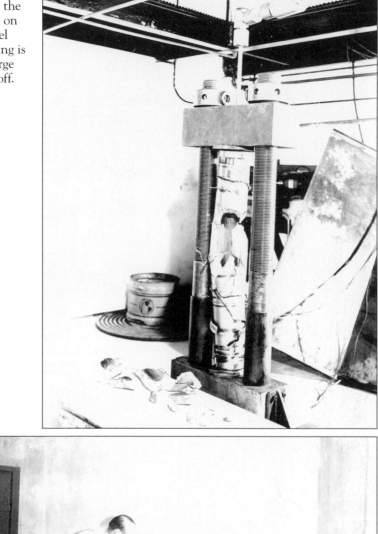

A scene at the laboratory showing a clever, but probably not-too-safe method for moving a "radium pill" (in other words, a radiation source), using fishing line.

This photograph shows large X-ray apparatus in use in building 45.

Date and identification were not available for this image, but it seems likely to have been another kind of radiological testing process.

Here Inspection School students get acquainted with the tools of the X-ray department.

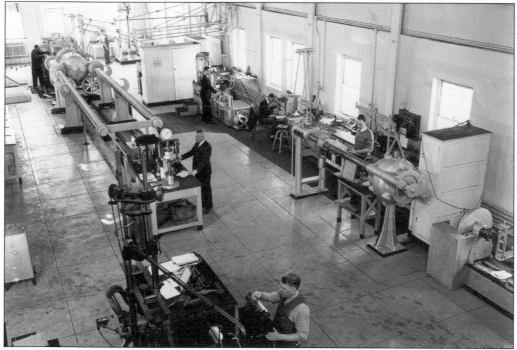

This is another view of the physical testing laboratory with the Emery Testing Machine toward the left.

On February 20, 1944, the Watertown Arsenal got national attention for producing its 100,000th artillery tube. Seen here practicing for the live broadcast of *Army Hour* on NBC are Lt. Col. William E. Slater, radio branch, war department, Bureau of Public Relations; announcer James F. Halloran (casting machine leader); and Col. John Mather, commanding officer, Watertown Arsenal.

A group of spectators crowds around the NBC broadcast engineers who are preparing for the *Army Hour* broadcast in the foundry.

In this image, a crowd wildly cheers the announcement that the metal has been successfully poured for the 100,000th gun tube.

Here spectators view the 100,000th gun tube, cast at the Watertown Arsenal using a special centrifugal process.

'Red Hot' Gun Barrel for Arme—

II, NO. 14 — THURSDAY, FEBRUARY 17, 1944 — WATERTOWN, MASS.

er Annum

uestionnaires
 Be Audited

# ARSENAL ON ARMY HOUR SUNDAY
## Casting of 100,000th Gun to Be Broadcast 'Round the World

NEW GUINEA TUNING IN—American troops like these sitting around a native hut 10,000 miles away will be tuned in to the Army Hour as it carries to the fighting men in every corner of the earth the dramatic story of the casting by the Arsenal of its 100,000th gun tube. Morale goes up as production figures mount.

**Program originating in Bldg. 421 to go over 135 U. S. stations and by short wave overseas**

Next Sunday afternoon the Army Hour program will carry the story of the pouring of the 100,000th gun tube made at the Arsenal by the centrifugal casting process. Originating in Bldg. 421, the program will be sent out over the 135 stations of the National Broadcasting Company's national hook-up and will go by short wave to every corner of the world.

It will take approximately six minutes of the hour's program, and will be heard sometime between 3:30 and 4 p.m. over station WBZ in Boston, Sunday, Feb. 20.

Three microphones will pick up the roar of the casting machines in Bldg. 421 as the metal is being poured for the casting of a 105mm gun, the 100,000th tube to be turned out by the centrifugal casting method.

Col. John Mather, Commanding Officer, and James F. Halloran, centrifugal casting machine operator and leader on the 8-4 shift will be heard on the program.

Newsreel and picture syndicate photographers have been invited to witness the event.

The National Broadcasting Co. will have a radio engineer and an announcer on hand to handle the broadcast. From the microphones in Bldg. 421, the program is piped over telephone lines to New York City where it is then broadcast via 135 stations throughout the country. A recording is made of the broadcast and the Office of War Information sends it by short wave over 10 East and West Coast stations beamed to carry the program to U. S. armed forces listening in at our outposts all over the world.

### Arsenal Has Played Major Role in World War II

The production of the 100,000th gun tube by the centrifugal casting process dramatizes a milestone in modern gun manufacture and focuses attention on the major role which the Watertown Arsenal has played in the manufacture of gun tubes in this war, as it has done in each war since it was founded in 1816 on orders from President James Madison.

#### CARRIED EARLY LOAD OF PRODUCTION ALONE

During 1940, one year before Pearl Harbor, a total of 1600 castings were produced—all that the equipment would allow. In the year and one-half following Pearl Harbor, as more machines were built and non-trained, annual production jumped twenty-six fold. Practically the entire Army gun tube program was successfully carried out by the Arsenal alone until, July, 1942, when private industry had converted sufficiently to pick up part of the load. By this time, the Arsenal production totalled more than 40,000 tubes. Up until early 1943, six months after industry got rolling on gun tubes, the Arsenal still carried a large portion of the total program. From July, '42 to February, '44, its casting machines turned out 60,000 guns to be shipped to armed forces at all fighting fronts.

#### PRIMARY FUNCTION IS DEVELOPMENT WORK

Even though the primary function of the Arsenal is that of a "pilot station," for experimental and development work in designs, materials and methods, it was responsible for the production of practically all of the modern gun tubes available to the Army during the two years immediately preceding the outbreak of this war—and in the production program as a whole the Arsenal has been one of the largest single producers of gun tubes in the country.

COL. JOHN MATHER, Commanding Officer, will be on program Sunday if sufficiently recovered from illness.

JIM HALLORAN, casting machine operator, a leader in Bldg. 421, will describe operations. Has brother in Army.

## Centrifugal Gun Casting Process Developed by Watertown Arsenal

Making guns by the centrifugal casting process is new to this war and is a development of the Watertown Arsenal. The late Brig. Gen. Tracy C. Dickson, former Commanding Officer at the Arsenal, was father of the centrifugal casting process as applied to gun manufacture. Seventeen years ago this process started to replace the earlier, slower method of making gun barrels by forging process.

#### FASTER AND CHEAPER

Years of research, development, designing and building its own casting machines, went into the development of this method, which produces gun barrels by pouring molten metal into a mold while spinning around at a great speed. The centrifugal force caused by this rotation throws the metal out from the center to the sides of the mold, thus forming the long, rough gun tube, and leaving a small hole down through the center of the tube.

The centrifugal casting method has proved to be cheaper, faster and uses less metal than any previously developed method of making guns up to a certain size. It is a flexible process, as guns of several

**(Continued on Page 3)**

"Overconfidence and complacency are among our deadliest enemies... That attitude on the part of anyone —government or management or labor—can lengthen the war: It can kill American boys."
—President Franklin D. Roosevelt

(See page 3 for remarks by Col. Breakefield)

By a Staff Photographer

#### Arsenal Turns Out 100,000th Gun Tube

In ceremonies which were radioed around the world on the Army Hour program yesterday, the Watertown Arsenal turned out the 100,000th gun tube by the centrifugal casting process. Top Grappler attached to an overhead crane picks up the red-hot gun barrel and carries it away to be buried in cinder pits for cooling. Electrically-heated furnaces in which steel and alloys are melted. Worker, clad in thick woolen shirt, and wearing helmet and asbestos gloves, stirs the molten metal, skims slag, and tests for proper heat.

## 100,000th Gun Tube Is Cast In Roar Heard Around World

With a roar heard 'round the world—by means of a national hook-up and short-wave radio cast—a stream of molten metal poured into a huge casting machine at the Watertown Arsenal yesterday, and the 100,000th gun tube to be made at this plant by the centrifugal process was well on its way to play an important role in World War II.

The complete process of casting the big 40mm, 90mm, and 105mm gun tubes by this method takes about two hours and a half from the time the cold metal is put into an electrically-heated furnace to be melted down until the red-hot cast gun tube emerges from the machine and is buried in cinders on the floor to cool.

Under the centrifugal casting process, molten metal is poured into a rapidly revolving horizontal mold. The centrifugal force of the rotation acts on the steel just as it would on a pail of water swung around one's head in a circle, forcing it out from the center. The process was developed after many years of research and experiment involving not only the mixture of the metal, but also the designing, building, and installing of the machines to do the work.

Halloran, a casting machine leader employed at the plant for the last four years, represented his fellow workers in the radio program. Because the process is such a lengthy one, only the actual pouring of the liquid metal into the casting machine was radioed around the world.

The operation took place in a huge foundry—a very long and high, but quite dark building with a bank of casting machines at each end of the dirt floor. Directly behind the casting machines and about 15 feet above them is the melting platform where the electrically-heated furnaces melt down the steel and alloys. There, also, the control equipment is located.

Previously, gun barrels—or gun tubes, as they are known technically—were made by the forging method, which had been used for a number of years. About 1926, the Army Ordnance centrifugal casting process became more prominent and emphasis was laid on this method of making gun tubes at the Watertown Arsenal.

During 1940, a total of only 1,600 gun tubes was produced at this ordnance plant by the casting method, this being all the equipment at that time would permit. In the year and a half following Pearl Harbor, annual production jumped 26-fold. By July, 1942, the Arsenal had produced more than 40,000 gun tubes, making the plant one of the largest single producers of such gun tubes in the entire country.

Yesterday, the 100,000th gun was cast, and a description of the operation was given during the "Army Hour" radio program, Col. John Mather, commanding officer

Hot
Loo

Late Maker Water the E evenin selling goers their t with c 51, or unsold hands. The very fi availai those will b cause the co be no dance

### Centrifugal Casting Contribution by Watertown Arsenal
**(Continued from Page 1)**

sizes can be produced in one machine merely by changing molds. Each casting unit is self-contained and requires but little floor space. All machines were designed, built and installed by Arsenal employees.

Although this method has already proved to be one of the major contributions to gun production in this war, development and experimentation with the process still goes on. The Arsenal is now constructing a new casting machine which if successful will be able to cast guns requiring almost four times as much metal as the 90mm gun tube which up to this time is the largest gun produced by this method. The new casting machine, under construction in Bldg. 41, is expected to be ready for trial runs sometime in late March or early April.

nday

adford, where ts Hotel Brad will do their o about 700

day-eve crowd d with many as guests of nd the Frolic fete a comple iecemen large out the party. ell as modern ved up in gen-

ing Men Dollars

10% or More?

City
Ma

WAT the world 100,000th arsenal metal po

Income Tax
Information

HUBbard 8500

EXTRA TAX PAYS AT
RSONNEL OFFICE

Another Arsenal Boy
Missing in Action

These press clippings, assembled by the Watertown Arsenal press office, show the amount of news that the event generated within the region including the *Boston Post, Boston Herald, Boston Globe, Boston Evening American, Boston Advertiser, Christian Science Monitor, New England*

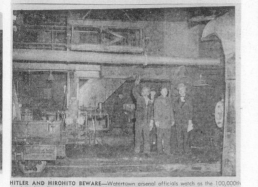

## ARSENAL CASTS 100,000th GUN

Dramatizing the role being played by the Watertown Arsenal in this war was the casting of the 100,000th gun there Sunday afternoon by the centrifugal casting process, new to this war, and which was developed by the arsenal.

The ceremony for the casting of the gun was extremely brief in order that as little time as possible be lost on the production line. Aiding in the casting of the gun was Jim Halloran, a casting machine operator, who has a brother in the army.

(Continued on Page 3)

## 100,000TH GUN TUBE IS CAST AT THE ARSENAL

### Roar Of Molten Metal Heard Around The World Sunday On Army Hour Broadcast Marking Event

With a roar heard 'round the world—by means of a national hookup and short-wave radiocast—a stream of molten metal surged into a huge casting machine at the Watertown Arsenal Sunday, and this 100,000th gun tube to be made at this plant by the centrifugal process was well on its way to play an important role in World War II.

The complete process of casting the big 105mm, 90mm, and 155mm gun tubes by the method takes about two hours and a half from the time the cold metal is put into the machine till the finished gun tube emerges from the machine and is buried in cinders on the floor to cool.

Under the centrifugal casting process, molten metal is poured into a rapidly revolving horizontal mold. The centrifugal force of the rotation acts on the steel just as it would in

(Continued on Page 3)

a pail of water swung around the center. The presence of the center years of development...

(Continued on Page 3)

## 100,000th Gun

(Continued from Page 1)

and experiment involving not the mixture of the metal, but the designing building, and tooling of the machines to do the...

Previously, gun barrel-or tubes, as they are known technically—were made by the forging method, which had been used a number of years. About 1918 Army Ordnance centrifugal...

## Watertown Arsenal Produces 100,000th Gun by New Method

Army ordnance engineers adopted the principle of the cream separator used in American dairies to produce at great speed enough cannon to stop the attacks of our enemies on every front. That principle is centrifugal force, first used successfully in the manufacture of gun barrels at the Watertown Arsenal.

The Watertown arsenal yesterday produced its 100,000th gun tube since 1940 by the centrifugal casting process, a record that would not have been possible under the forging process formerly used.

The centrifugal process, a new development, made it possible for the arsenal to manufacture 60,000 gun barrels in a little more than a year and a half, since July, 1942, as compared to a total production of 40,000 gun tubes from 1940 to this time. During 1940, the arsenal produced 1600 castings by this method. A year and one-half after Pearl Harbor, this rate had been increased twenty-six fold.

The casting of the 100,000th barrel, a 105mm type, was dramatized yesterday in the "Army Hour" radio program over a nation-wide hook-up of 135 radio stations and beamed by short-wave to our troops in every corner of the world. Three microphones recorded the roar of the casting machine as it turned out the gun barrel.

Col. John Mather, commanding officer, and James P. Halloran, centrifugal casting machine operator, explained the process.

The centrifugal casting process for gun tubes was initiated by Brig. Gen. Tracy C. Dickson, former commanding officer of the arsenal from 1918 to 1922. About 1936, this process had reached a high state of development and was being employed widely at the Watertown Arsenal.

Several sizes of tubes can be produced in a single casting machine merely by changing molds.

Arsenal officials also are hopeful that the method can be applied to the manufacture of guns requiring almost four times as much metal as the 90mm gun tube.

**100,000TH GUN.** The 100,000th gun made by the centrifugal process at the Watertown Arsenal is shown above in the process of manufacture. Col. John Mather, commanding officer of the Arsenal, watches as James Halloran, Worcester, stamps the "100,000th" on the 76-mm. dual tank and anti-tank gun as it emerges from the mold. The process was originated and developed there.

## ARSENAL CASTS 100,000TH GUN

### Simple Ceremony Marks Watertown Affair

Dramatizing the role being played by the Watertown Arsenal in this war was the casting of the 100,000th gun there yesterday afternoon by the centrifugal casting process, new to this war and which was developed by the arsenal.

The ceremony for the casting of the gun was extremely brief in that so little time as possible be lost on the production line. Aiding in the casting of the gun was Jim Halloran, a casting machine operator, who has a brother in the Army.

...eye of Col. John Mather, commanding ...n Arsenal, James F. Halloran of Wor... operator, stamps number 100,000 on a ...barrel as it comes out of the furnace. ...l Harbor, the equipment would allow, ...an increased until the present record of ...ings was set. (Associated Press Photo)

## Broadcasts of Gun Tube

...20—(AP)—Soldiers and sailors all over ...y shortwave radio the making of the ...e centrifugal process at the Watertown ...e picked up the roar when the hot...

The centrifugal casting process ...is one by which molten steel is ...poured into a rapidly revolving ...horizontal mold and permits far ...more rapid production than the ...and drop forge method of making ...gun barrels, plant officials said.

Because it developed the centrifugal casting process, officials said, the Watertown arsenal "has carried a very large portion of the wartime mass production burden of making gun barrels."

## Gun Tube

Continued from Page One

James F. Halloran, 135 Dewey street, Worcester, a casting machine leader, was the employe speaker on the radio program broadcast by NBC.

James F. Halloran, who lives with his father, William J. Halloran, commutes between Worcester and his Watertown...

## Arsenal's 100,000th Gun

### WATERTOWN ARSENAL
## Casting Of 100,000th Gun Is Broadcast On Army Hour

The Army Hour program carried the story Sunday of the pouring of the 100,000th gun tube made at the Watertown Arsenal by the centrifugal casting process. Originating in Bldg. 421, the program was sent out over the 135 stations of the National Broadcasting Company's national hook-up and by short wave to every corner of the world.

Three microphones picked up the gun tube by the centrifugal casting process dramatizes a milestone in modern gun manufacture and focuses attention on the major role which the Watertown Arsenal has played in the manufacture of gun tubes in this war, as it has done in each war. It was founded in 1816 on orders from President James Madison.

During 1940, one year before Pearl Harbor, a total of 1600 castings were produced—all that the equipment would allow. In the...

Col. John Mather, Commanding Officer, and James F. Halloran, centrifugal casting machine operator and leader on the 8-4 shift, were heard on the program.

The production of the 100,000th...

---

*Minuteman, Watertown Herald, Watertown Tribune-Enterprise,* and the *Worcester Telegram.* The story in the *Arsenal News* concentrated particularly on the work of casting machine operator James Halloran, who had a brother in the service.

One picture is worth a thousand words. This image shows thousands of 37-millimeter gun tubes, stacked outside of the Watertown Arsenal's buildings.

This April 1945 image shows a 240-millimeter shell being spray-painted in a ventilated booth.

Here a Watertown Arsenal worker is handling the movement and storage of hundreds of 240-millimeter shells.

A captured German Mark IV medium tank offered Watertown Arsenal workers an opportunity to see what they were up against and a chance to pitch savings programs. The sign on the tank reads, "The Mighty 7th War Loan Cavalcade, sponsored by the Savings Banks of Mass. in cooperation with the U.S. Treasury and the U.S. Army." The fact that this image is probably from late in the war is shown by the image on the poster at the front of the trailer, inspired by the 1945 flag raising on Iwo Jima.

Ingenuity was encouraged at the Watertown Arsenal. Here E. J. Maroney, author of suggestion 4491, demonstrates his invention: a hydraulic lift for hitching gun carriages to pintle hooks on tow vehicles.

This dramatic image shows molten metal being poured into molds in the foundry.

# *Five*

# THE NUCLEAR AGE

This interesting post–World War II image has no identifying information but seems to be some kind of Watertown Arsenal demonstration of gun sighting techniques.

Safety seems to have been a major focus of attention after the war, perhaps because production was no longer quite so urgent a matter.

With the emphasis on encouraging safer practices among individuals, this accident doghouse served as a reminder of personal responsibility.

Tuberculosis remained a major public health threat after World War II. This mobile X-ray van is paying a visit to the Watertown Arsenal in 1946.

Employees were encouraged to avoid accidents off the job too. Here Watertown Arsenal leaders and Massachusetts Registry of Motor Vehicles personnel team up. From left to right are Capt. O. B. Gomer, industrial relations officer; A. E. Cowie, director of training; Alfred T. Little, supervisor of safety education at the Massachusetts registry; Col. Carroll M. Deitrick, commanding officer; and Robert Panora, safety education instructor at the Massachusetts registry. Panora later became head of the registry in the 1970s.

The safety theme was further hammered home in a series of exhibits. Here the strength of the steel toe inserts used in protective boots is demonstrated by supporting the front wheels of a truck.

Two men discuss the broken and bent tools on the board. Whether these were being shown as causes or results of accidents is not known.

This young boy seems especially impressed with this poster of the hidden picture variety, warning of off-the-job hazards.

The main gate prepares to welcome open house visitors around 1950.

The main gate is viewed here from an interior vantage point. A late model Studebaker has just crossed the tracks on its way out of the Watertown Arsenal.

Here is another view of the same location, apparently during a warmer season, judging by the awning that has been deployed over the guardhouse door.

Here a distinguished-looking group, identities unknown, tours a machine shop at the Watertown Arsenal.

The two boys in the foreground seem to be very impressed—perhaps by the Emery Testing Machine—in what appears to be a testing laboratory.

Commanding officer Carroll Deitrick is at the center of this discussion involving blue prints and more. Judging by the signage on the right, the event had something to do with procurement.

This is another open house shot, with visitors touring the turret lathe section of the shops.

A later model of the World War II Sherman tank, with the longer 76-millimeter gun, is climbing off its tank transporter vehicle for the benefit of open house visitors.

Here visitors take a closer look at the tank, which would have been reaching the end of its United States service life at this point.

Visitors were free to explore the inner workings of this turretless Sherman tank.

This broader view of the equipment on display shows a few Shermans to the left. A tank transporter to the right and a more modern turret, without a hull, in the center, near the building.

Another of the Watertown Arsenal's illustrious visitors was five-star general Douglas MacArthur. Here the officers of the Watertown Arsenal prepare to impress the general, who had recently been dismissed from his command in Korea. He was thought by many to be considering a run for the presidency.

From left to right, C. A. McCarthy, P. E. Johanson, and M. Shields inspect the plaque made for MacArthur by the Watertown Arsenal.

Watertown Arsenal records indicated that the four people standing before the Arsenal gate, awaiting the arrival of Gen. Douglas MacArthur, are, from left to right, Lieutenant Heemstra, Miss Culkeen, Col. Carroll Deitrick, and Mrs. Deitrick.

MacArthur's motorcade is seen here passing through Watertown on the way to the Watertown Arsenal. The general is in the back seat.

Col. Carroll Deitrick salutes and greets MacArthur upon his arrival at the Watertown Arsenal.

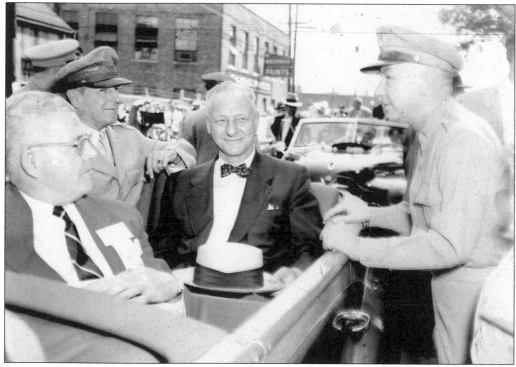

Here Deitrick has opened a conversation with his visitors. MacArthur is beaming from the back seat.

Next in line to greet Gen. Douglas MacArthur were the ladies.

Underscoring MacArthur's popularity at the time, the man sitting in front of him bears a badge that identifies him as a member of the MacArthur Committee.

MacArthur eventually got out of his limousine and pressed the flesh at the Watertown Arsenal gate and elsewhere in the facility.

This 1951 photograph shows the graduation of three apprentices from the four-year apprentice machinist course. From left to right are graduates Louis Frongillo, Frank Buonomo, and Barton Waldo, along with Capt. Richard A. Unger, industrial relations officer; Capt. Dale A. Duval, training officer; and Allen E. Cowie, director of training.

This photograph shows some heavy lifting in progress, involving a track-mounted crane and a smaller, motorized unit. Perhaps this is a prototype for the Atomic Cannon gun carriage (see page 124).

For many years, the army operated its own locomotive on the extensive trackage within the Watertown Arsenal. The son of a researcher, commissioned as an army officer, who lived at the Watertown Arsenal during and shortly after World War II, recalls that a prank he and a playmate dreamed up—seeing what kinds of things the locomotive could crush—inadvertently led to the locomotive derailing.

A dramatic photograph shows sparks and molten debris being emitted by one of the Watertown Arsenal's furnaces.

This similarly dramatic shot may show a welding operation in process.

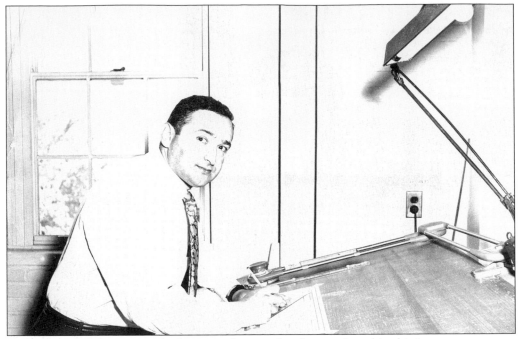

An unidentified designer or draftsman is shown at his drawing board in this image.

Here the same individual seems to be posing, probably with items he helped design.

Col. Carroll Deitrick is seen here at his desk. The colonel later earned the rank of brigadier general before departing the Watertown Arsenal.

Here Deitrick honors a shop employee.

This man is identified in the National Archive collections as Dr. Kostling.

The activity here is unknown, but the two men in this chemical laboratory seem to be cooking up something fun, judging by the smiles on their faces.

A group of men poses here with a gun
and mount. Judging by its high traverse, it
is probably an antiaircraft weapon.

Col. Carroll Deitrick (second from left) and colleagues seem to be on an inspection tour.

This group is admiring the controls of a 75-millimeter M51 Skysweeper antiaircraft gun, which the Watertown Arsenal helped develop. This was a very advanced weapon for its day with automatic ammunition loading and a built-in radar and analog computer for tracking targets. A few were hurriedly deployed to Korea.

An undated group photograph from the Watertown Arsenal files shows employees from many different functions, along with two officers at the center of the front row.

W. J. McMahon is shown here using counting equipment (manufactured by Tracer Lab, an early Route 128 high-tech company) in the Watertown Arsenal Isotope Laboratory, on May 13, 1953.

In this photograph, also from May 13, 1953, Herbert Campbell is making adjustments to some electroplating equipment.

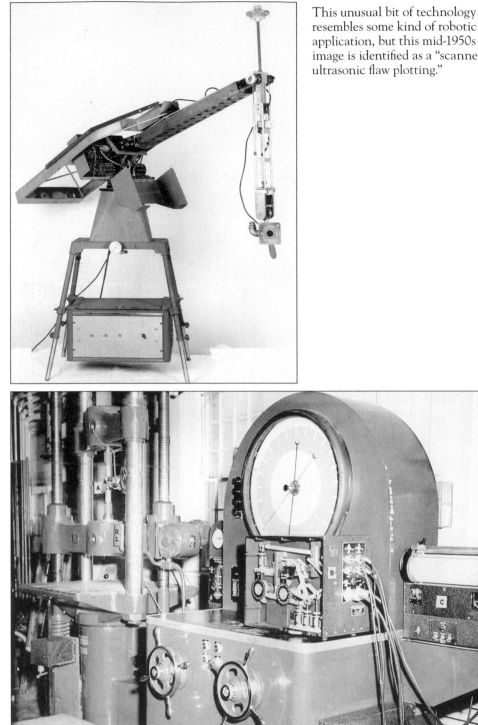

This unusual bit of technology resembles some kind of robotic application, but this mid-1950s image is identified as a "scanner for ultrasonic flaw plotting."

This photograph shows a "true stress-true strain test set up." At the far left is the diameter measurement unit. The box in front of the large dial is the computer (although not in the modern sense), and the unit at the far right is the chart recorder.

A Watertown Arsenal staff member is shown here performing vacuum fusion gas analysis, a process that could be used to find very small quantities of gases in substances such as metals.

This May 13, 1953, photograph shows John Coulter making an adjustment on a bore scope, a device for making optical inspections of inaccessible areas, such as the inside of a tube or gun barrel.

The protective gear on the workers is due to the fact that this area was the experimental uranium melt laboratory.

Again these Watertown Arsenal workers are swathed in extra protective gear because they are performing experimental tests on forging methods for uranium.

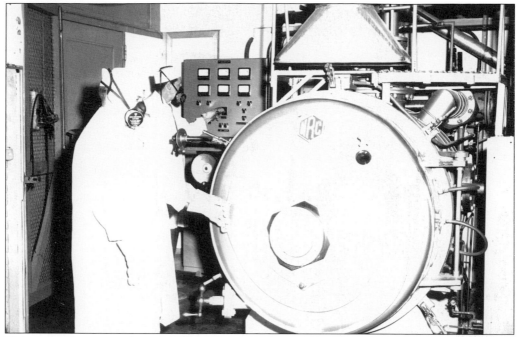

This is another view of a uranium processing activity. The Watertown Arsenal experimented with grinding, melting, and forging uranium.

This high angle photograph, shows crowds at an open house along with the same machine shown on page 84.

And what about when it came time to dispose of hazardous uranium? The state of the art in the mid-1950s was not very advanced. This image is described as the "burning site for uranium scrap"—simply a collection of barrels. Combustion was probably aided by the addition of petroleum. Note the presence of houses a short distance away.

This image is described as the "Cold Working Department." A large rotary saw is visible in the center of the image.

This is a 1956 cutaway view of the research reactor planned for the Watertown Arsenal. The project was in part an outgrowth of radiographic testing research by arsenal employee Dr. Horace Hardy Lester, for whom the reactor was ultimately named (posthumously).

This October 1959 image shows the containment structure for the nuclear reactor nearly completed. The reactor cost $1.35 million. Vara Construction of Boston performed the work under the direction of the U.S. Army Corps of Engineers.

While the containment vessel was essentially complete in October 1959, much work remained to be done. This inside view shows the airlock and other construction activity.

A balcony view of the interior of the containment building shows extensive continuing work.

The reactor, shown here completed, was dedicated on May 17, 1960. The reactor was used until about 1970 and was decommissioned under the jurisdiction of the Nuclear Regulatory Commission in 1992. The structure was demolished in 1994.

This Brighton view of the Watertown Arsenal, probably from the mid-1950s, shows the short-lived antiaircraft battery, equipped with 120-millimeter guns, that was set up do defend the Watertown Arsenal from possible attack by Soviet bombers. The location is near the present-day skating rink.

This image and the one below, both from 1961, were taken by Merritt Nesin while stationed in Germany. They show the 280-millimeter cannon of the 3rd Battlion, 82nd Artillery, 5th Corps, during training with the 3rd Armored Division at Grafenwoehr, Germany. Both images appear courtesy of Nesin and the 3rd Armored Division Web-site.

Better known as the Atomic Cannon, for their ability to fire either a conventional round or an atomic round, similar in power to the Hiroshima bomb, these guns were first fielded in the early 1950s and were retired in 1963. They were probably the largest road artillery ever made, with a powered tractor at each end. Watertown designed and built the carriage, and Watervliet Arsenal in New York manufactured the gun tubes.

With buildings of the Watertown Arsenal in the background, this 1962 image shows a standard M52 tractor truck towing a Watertown Arsenal–developed XM67 Sergeant Missile launcher, in traveling position.

This XM289 launcher for the "Honest John" tactical nuclear missile was brought to completion in only 11 months.

The Watertown Arsenal designed and built this enclosed litter for this variant of the Sikorsky S-51 for evacuating wounded.

This photograph from July 11, 1962, shows the equipment of the Watertown Arsenal fire department.

# ed Closed By Defense Sec. McNamara

## ARSENAL EMPLOYEES SHOCKED BY DEFENSE SECRETARY'S ORDER

Without any advance warning, and with thunderclap force, the announcement was made on Friday the 24th of April 1964, that the Secretary of Defense had directed the closing of Watertown Arsenal.

The announcement in itself was enough to shock all concerned, but when it was coupled with such innuendos as "obsolete" and "unneeded" the pride of the work force in its work and the Arsenal created a violent counteraction.

How could we be considered obsolete if we were doing work that no one else could or would handle at the time? How could we be considered obsolete if we had been undergoing a modernization of facilities and acquiring the latest in numerically controlled machine tools? How could we be considered obsolete when we had just finished converting to an RCA electronic computer for processing data? How could we be considered unneeded if we were using processes on items not yet mastered by other Arsenals or industry in general? How could we be considered unneeded if our delivery schedules were so tight, we had to operate on three shifts for some work?

### Went Home Dazed

With all these unanswered ques-

## *Surprise Statement Stuns Arsenal Employees*

Colonel Jordahn, Commanding Officer at the Watertown Arsenal, issued the following statement to all Arsenal employees on 24 April 1964:

"Secretary of Defense Robert S. McNamara today announced 63 actions to consolidate, reduce or discontinue Department of Defense activities in the United States and overseas. Fifty-five of these actions affect military activities in 29 states. The remaining eight affect overseas activities. When completed, the actions will produce annual savings of $68 million and reduce personnel by 10,056 without in any way reducing military effectiveness. The actions announced today resulted from the accelerated study of Defense Installations directed by President Johnson in December. The 63 actions place primary stress upon consolidation of related activities within and among the military departments and the Defense Supply Agency (DSA) in order to reduce overhead costs and facilities.

### Disposal By September 1967

Of most pertinence to us is the following announcement: At Watertown Arsenal, Watertown, Massachusetts, activities are to be phased out and Watertown Arsenal is to be declared excess and reported to GSA for disposal by September 1967, except for the facilities to be occupied by Army Materials Research Agency which will remain at Watertown. Personnel savings of 13 military and 1,836 civilians and annual dollar savings of $5.3 million are expected. All career employees whose jobs are eliminated will be offered other job opportunities. Normal attrition in the work force will provide job opportunities for considerable numbers of those affected by the closing. By careful advance planning and of hiring freezes additional jobs will be made available for the others involved in the cutback.

If the new job offered an employee requires a move to another defense installation, the moving expenses involved will be borne by the government. To assure the widest opportunity for new jobs retraining programs for skills required with the Defense Department will be established when necessary at Government expense".

The Commanding Officer will keep employees fully informed on all instructions he receives.

This clip from the *Arsenal News* tells of the shock and dismay that greeted the unexpected decision in 1964 by Secretary of Defense Robert S. McNamara to close the arsenal.

# Across America, People are Discovering Something Wonderful. Their Heritage.

Arcadia Publishing is the leading local history publisher in the United States. With more than 3,000 titles in print and hundreds of new titles released every year, Arcadia has extensive specialized experience chronicling the history of communities and celebrating America's hidden stories, bringing to life the people, places, and events from the past. To discover the history of other communities across the nation, please visit:

## www.arcadiapublishing.com

Customized search tools allow you to find regional history books about the town where you grew up, the cities where your friends and family live, the town where your parents met, or even that retirement spot you've been dreaming about.